CONTENTS

ISBN: 9780170354196

Formulae

These are the formulae for this achievement standard. Remember to check with your teacher to see which ones you will be provided with in your assessment.

Midpoint of a line	$\left(\frac{x_1 + x_2}{2}, \frac{y_1 + y_2}{2}\right)$
Distance between two points	$d = \sqrt{(x_2 - x_1)^2 + (y_2 - y_1)^2}$
Gradient of a line	$m = \frac{y_2 - y_1}{x_2 - x_1}$
Parallel lines	$m_1 = m_2$
Perpendicular lines	$m_1 \times m_2 = -1$
Equation of a line — basic	$y = mx + c$
Equation of a line — given a gradient and a point	$y - y_1 = m(x - x_1)$

ISBN: 9780170354196

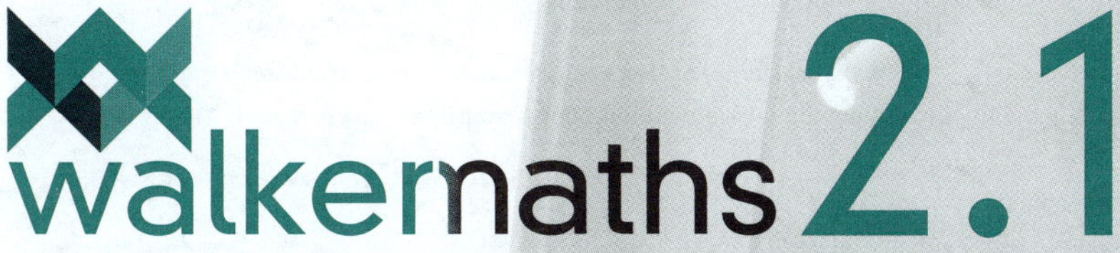

CO-ORDINATE GEOMETRY

NCEA Level 2 Internal

Charlotte Walker and Victoria Walker

Walker Maths 2.1 Co-ordinate Geometry
1st Edition
Charlotte Walker
Victoria Walker

Editor: Eva Chan
Cover and Text design: Cheryl Smith, Macarn Design
Production controller: Siew Han Ong
Reprint: Jess Lovell

Acknowledgements
Cover photo courtesy of Shutterstock.

We wish to thank the Boards of Trustees of Darfield and Riccarton High Schools for allowing us to use materials and ideas developed while teaching. Our thanks also go to all past and present colleagues who have generously shared their experience and ideas.

For product information and technology assistance,
in Australia call **1300 790 853**;
in New Zealand call **0800 449 725**

For permission to use material from this text or product, please email **aust.permissions@cengage.com**

National Library of New Zealand Cataloguing-in-Publication Data
A catalogue record for this book is available from the National Library of New Zealand.

ISBN 978 0 17 035419 6

Cengage Learning Australia
Level 7, 80 Dorcas Street
South Melbourne, Victoria Australia 3205

For learning solutions, visit **cengage.co.nz**

Printed in China by 1010 Printing International Limited.
21 26 25

Glossary

Make your own glossary of key terms:

Term	Definition	Picture/Example
Midpoint		
Length		
Gradient		
General equation		
Perpendicular		
Parallel		
Intersection		
Bisector		
Diagonal		
Vertex (plural: vertices)		

ISBN: 9780170354196

Term	Definition	Picture/Example
Collinear points		
Equilateral triangle		
Isosceles triangle		
Scalene triangle		
Right-angled triangle		
Incentre		
Circumcentre		
Orthocentre		
Mediator		
Bisector		
Perpendicular bisector		
Origin		

ISBN: 9780170354196

Co-ordinates revision

Write down the co-ordinates of the lettered points shown below.
Remember: the *x* co-ordinate comes first, then the *y* co-ordinate, (*x*, *y*).

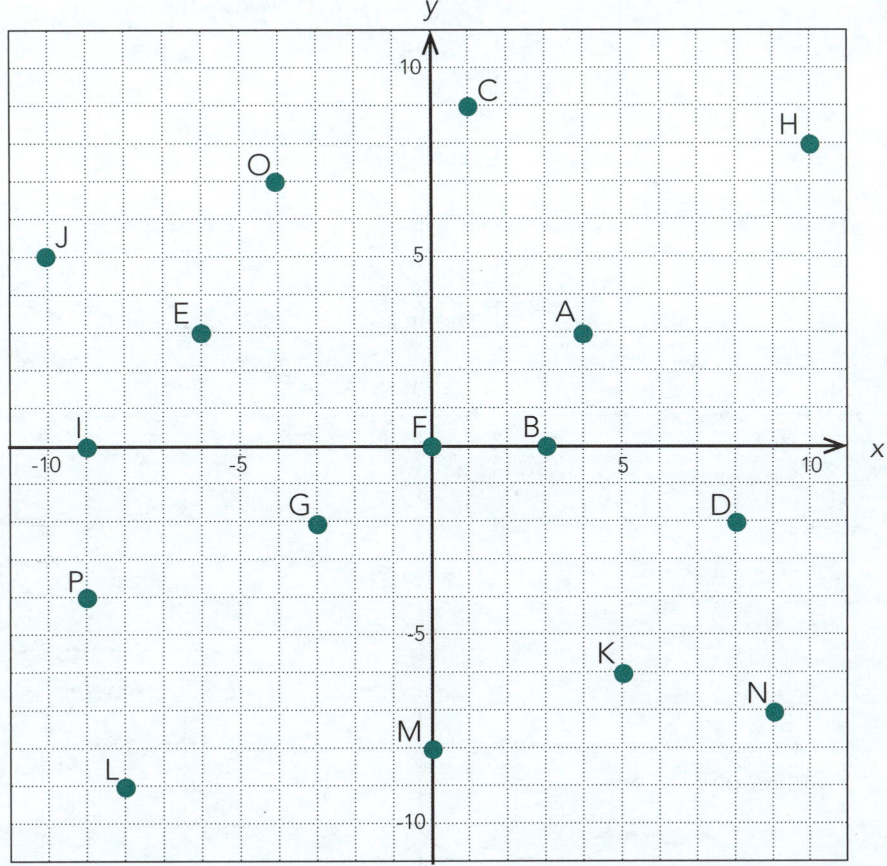

A (,) B (,)

C (,) D (,)

E (,) F (,)

G (,) H (,)

I (,) J (,)

K (,) L (,)

M (,) N (,)

O (,) P (,)

ISBN: 9780170354196

Plot and label the following co-ordinate points on the grid below.

A	(2, 5)	B	(-7, 2)
C	(-3, 10)	D	(1, -8)
E	(10, 5)	F	(-5 , -3)
G	(-3, -7)	H	(5 , -4)
I	(4, 9)	J	(-9, 8)
K	(6, 0)	L	(-8, -7)
M	(4, -9)	N	(-5, 6)
O	(0, -3)	P	(-6, -9)

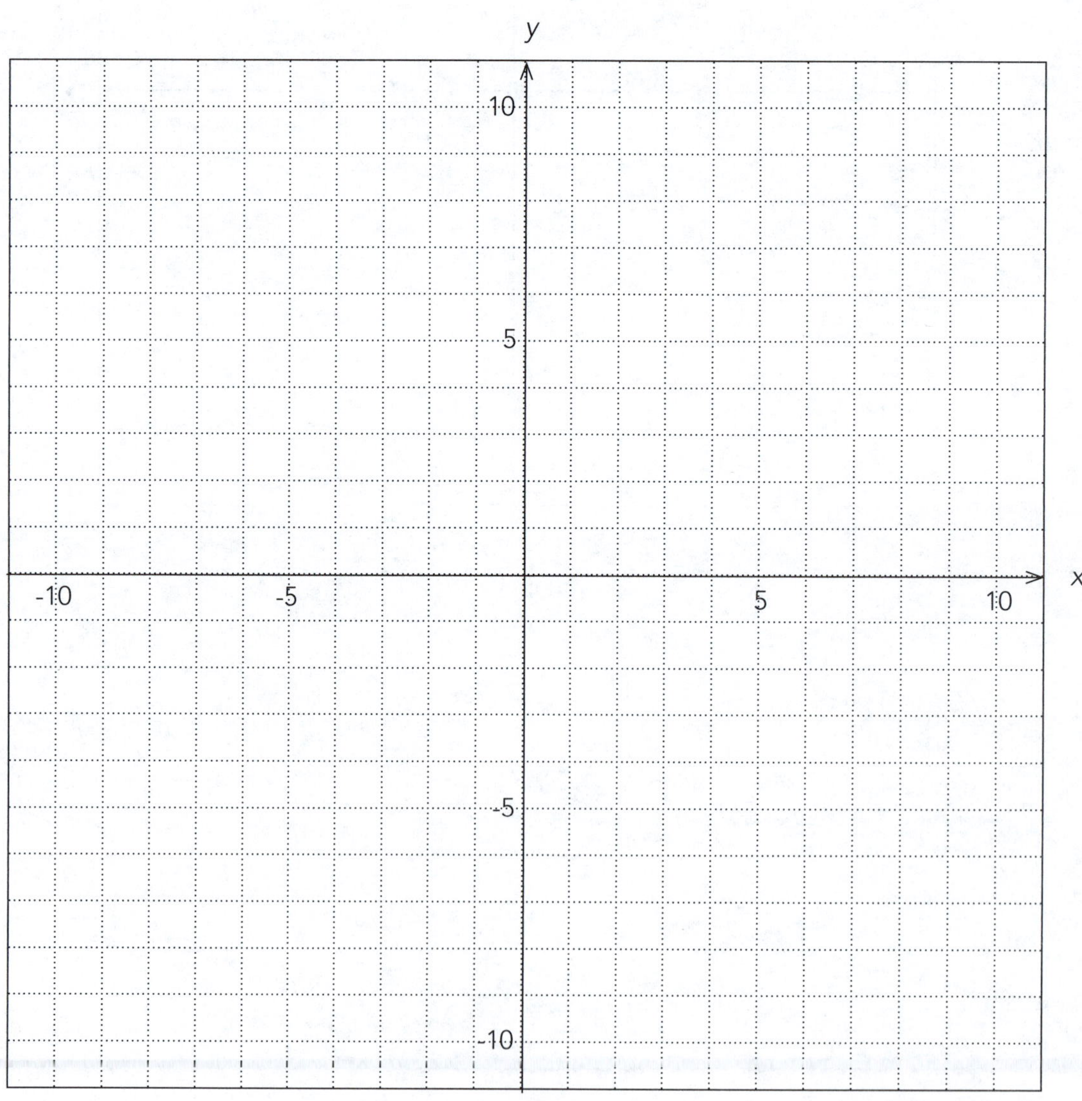

  ISBN: 9780170354196

Midpoints

Using the formula $\left(\frac{x_1 + x_2}{2}, \frac{y_1 + y_2}{2}\right)$ we can calculate the midpoint of a line.

Example: Calculate the midpoint of a line joining the points (-5, 2) and (7, -6).

x_1 y_1 x_2 y_2

Midpoint $= \left(\frac{-5 + 7}{2}, \frac{2 + (-6)}{2}\right)$

$= (1, -2)$

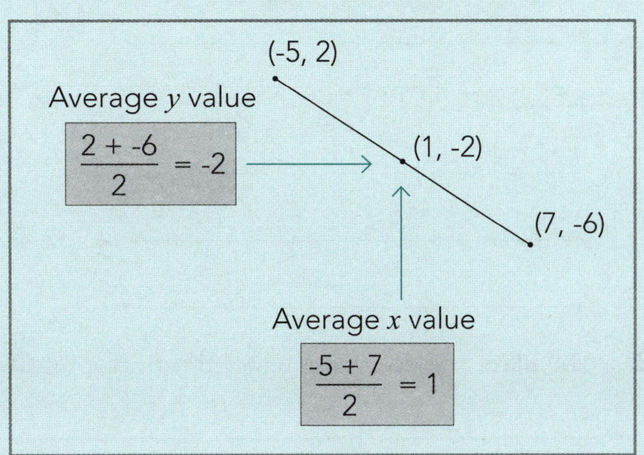

Calculate the midpoints of these lines.

1 (5, 8) and (7, 12)

2 (9, 6) and (1, 2)

3 (3, 11) and (9, 8)

4 (4, 0) and (12, 2)

5 (-3, 5) and (7, 1)

6 (2, -9) and (-4, 3)

ISBN: 9780170354196

7 (-6, -5) and (-2, 5)

8 (-4, 20) and (9, 3)

9 (-11, 0) and (2, -15)

10 (1, -7) and (-1, 10)

11 (3.5, 2) and (4, 1.5)

12 (-10.2, 1.8) and (-3.4, -5.2)

13 Calculate the co-ordinates of the midpoint of the line joining (4, -11) and (-2, 7).

14 The vertices of a triangle are P (-6,1), Q (2, 7) and R (6, -3). Calculate the midpoint of each side.

ISBN: 9780170354196

15 If the points X (-2, 1) and Y (4, -2) are the ends of the diameter of a circle, calculate the co-ordinates of the centre.

16 The midpoint of line AB is (4, 2). If the co-ordinates of A are (-3, -7), calculate the co-ordinates of B.

17 The point (19, -95) is the centre of a circle which has a diameter CD. If the co-ordinates of C are (p, -57) and the co-ordinates of D are (114, q), calculate the values of p and q.

18 Points E, F, G and H are spaced at equal intervals along a straight line. If E is (e, -26), F is (-65, 1), G is (-13, g) and H is (h, 55), calculate the values of e, g and h.

ISBN: 9780170354196

The distance between two points

Using the formula $d = \sqrt{(x_2 - x_1)^2 + (y_2 - y_1)^2}$ (actually Pythagoras's theorem) we can calculate the distance between two points.

Example: Calculate the length of a line joining the points (4, 5) and (-6, -3).

x_1 y_1 x_2 y_2

$$d = \sqrt{(-6 - 4)^2 + (-3 - 5)^2}$$
$$= \sqrt{(-10)^2 + (-8)^2}$$
$$= 12.81 \text{ (2 dp)}$$

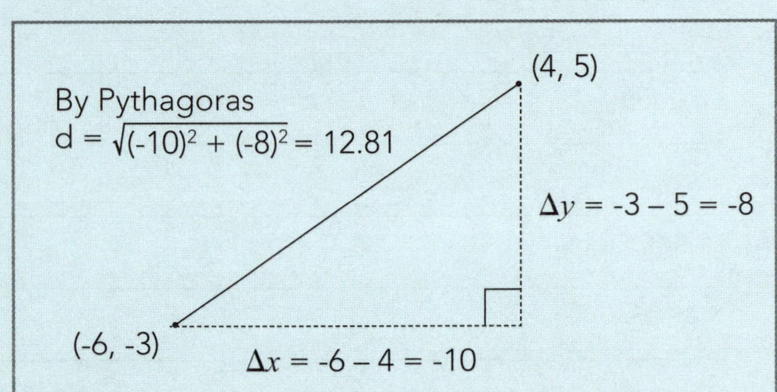

Calculate the distance between the following pairs of points.

1 (5, 8) and (7, 12)

2 (9, 6) and (1, 2)

3 (3, 11) and (9, 8)

4 (4, 0) and (12, 2)

5 (-3, 5) and (7, 1)

6 (2, -9) and (-4, 3)

ISBN: 9780170354196

7 (-6, -5) and (-2, 5)

8 (-4, 20) and (9, 3)

9 (-11, 0) and (2, -15)

10 (1, -7) and (-1, 10)

11 (1.75, 4.4) and (2.9, 7.8)

12 (-57, 91) and (18, -155)

13 The points A (-5, 5), B (6, 8) and C (9,-3) form the vertices of a triangle. Calculate the length of each side. Is this triangle scalene, isosceles or equilateral?

14 Calculate the distance of the point (7, -3) from the origin.

ISBN: 9780170354196

15 Three of the four points K (-6, 4), L (2, 5), M (2, -2) and N (-5, -3) lie on the circumference of a circle whose centre is O (-2, 1).

a Which point is not on the circumference? Justify your answer.

b Calculate the diameter of the circle.

16 A triangle has the vertices A (-51, 34), B (-136, -119) and C (153, -68). Calculate the length of each side. Is this triangle scalene, isosceles or equilateral?

17 The points P (-3, y) and Q (1, -3) form the ends of a 5 cm straight line. Calculate the two possible values of y.

18 Calculate the distance between (91, 65) and (143, 104).

 ISBN: 9780170354196

The gradient of a line

The gradient is the steepness, or slope, of a line.

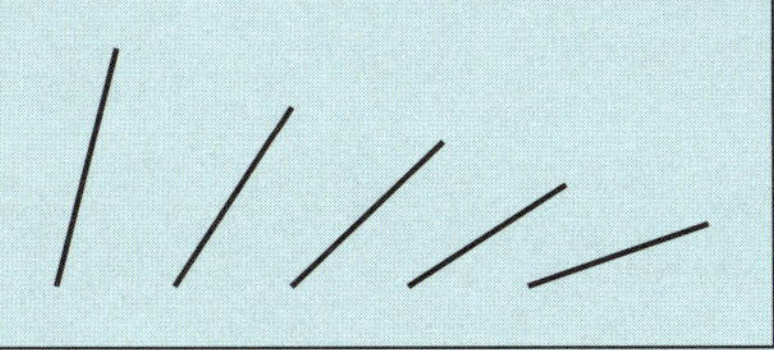

These lines all have positive gradients.

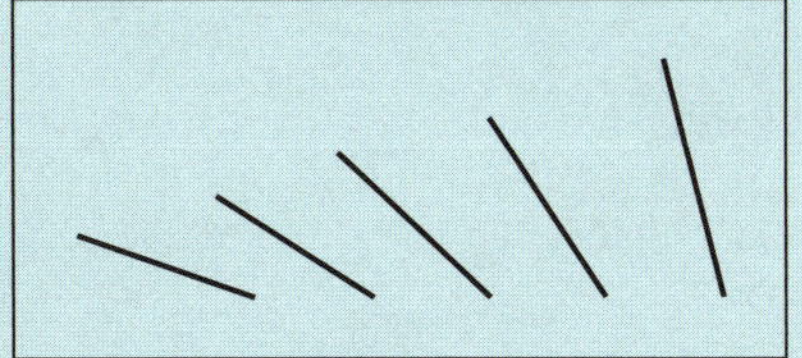

These lines all have negative gradients.

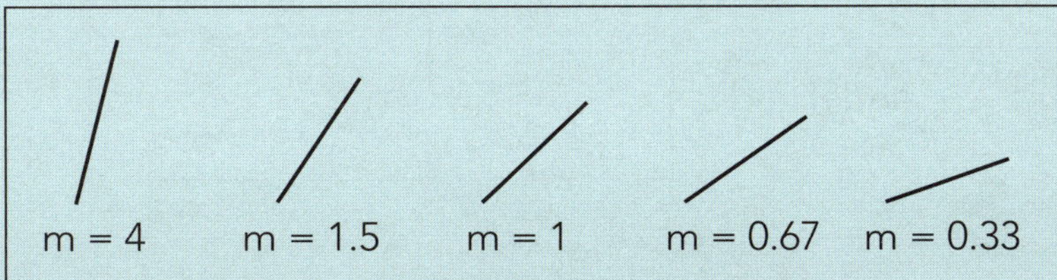

The steeper the line, the bigger the gradient.

The gradient is calculated using the formula $m = \frac{\text{change in } y}{\text{change in } x}$ or $\frac{\text{rise}}{\text{run}}$.

The easiest way to do this is to draw a right-angled triangle on the line.

$m = \frac{\text{rise}}{\text{run}}$

$= \frac{5}{6}$

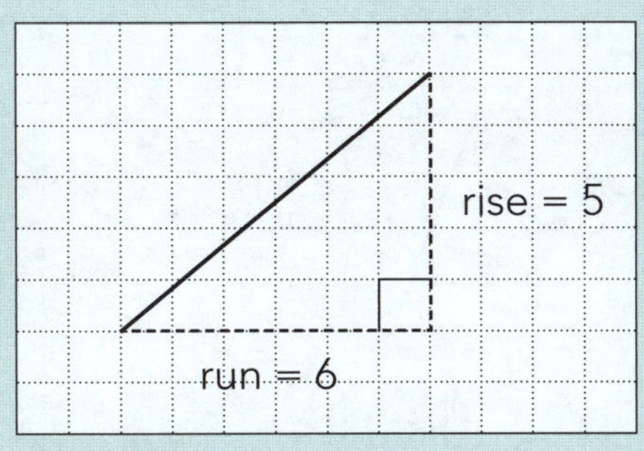

This time the gradient is *negative*.

$m = -\frac{\text{rise}}{\text{run}}$

$= -\frac{3}{7}$

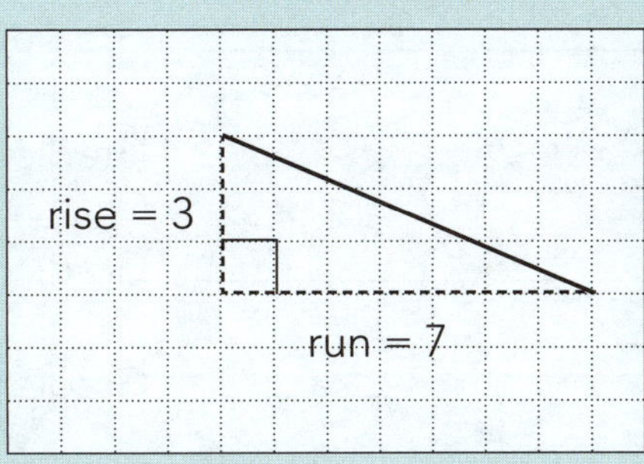

ISBN: 9780170354196

Horizontal lines

$$m = \frac{\text{rise}}{\text{run}}$$

$$= \frac{0}{7}$$

$$= 0$$

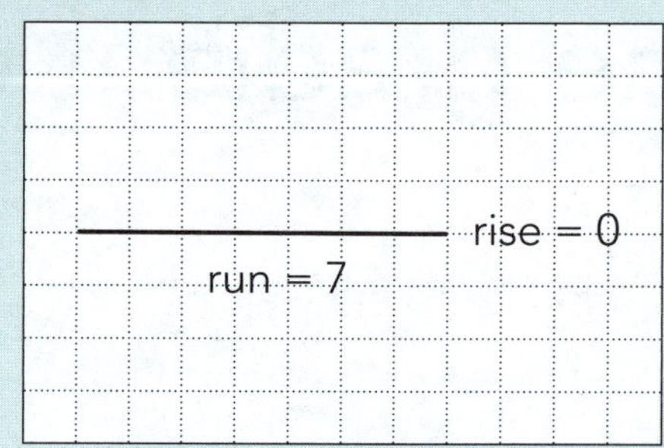

Vertical lines

$$m = \frac{\text{rise}}{\text{run}}$$

$$= \frac{5}{0}$$

$$= \text{undefined}$$

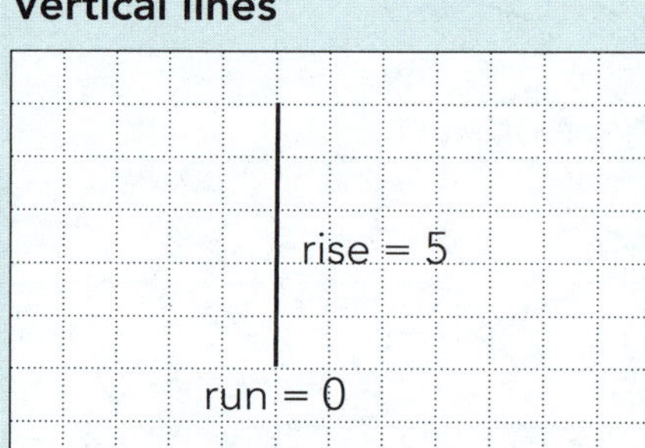

Calculate the gradients of these lines.

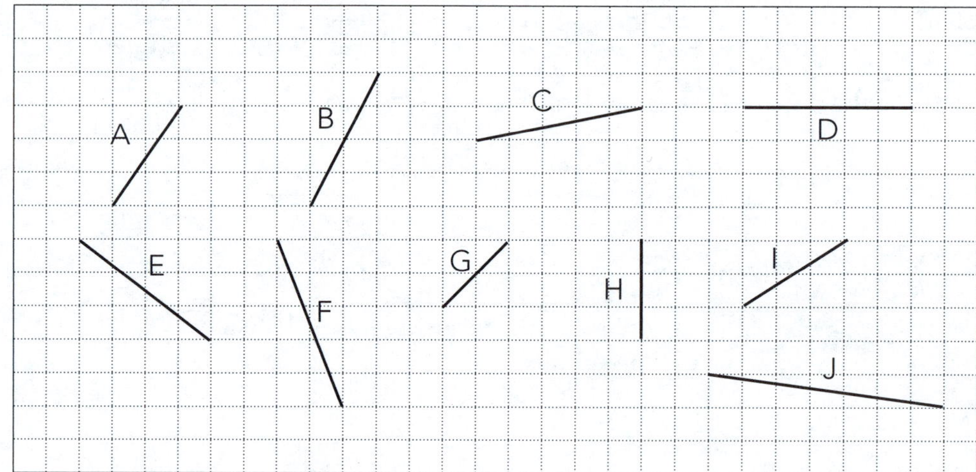

Gradient A = ______________________ Gradient B = ______________________

Gradient C = ______________________ Gradient D = ______________________

Gradient E = ______________________ Gradient F = ______________________

Gradient G = ______________________ Gradient H = ______________________

Gradient I = ______________________ Gradient J = ______________________

ISBN: 9780170354196

Draw line segments to show these gradients.

$A = \frac{1}{2}$ $B = 2$

$C = \frac{2}{5}$ $D = -1\frac{1}{2}$

$E = \frac{3}{7}$ $F = -\frac{5}{9}$

$G = -5$ $H = -1$

$I = 0$ $J = 3$

ISBN: 9780170354196

Calculating the gradient

Often you need to calculate the gradient *without* drawing the line.

We do this using the formula $m = \frac{y_2 - y_1}{x_2 - x_1}$

Example: Calculate the gradient of a line joining the points (-2, 5) and (1, -6).

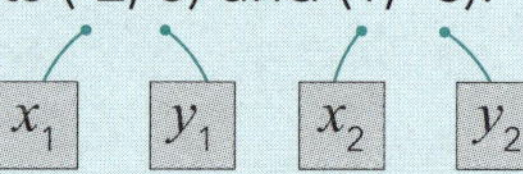

$$m = \frac{-6 - 5}{1 - (-2)} = -\frac{11}{3}$$

Calculate the gradient of the line connecting the following pairs of points.

1 (5, 8) and (7 ,12)

2 (9, 6) and (1, 2)

3 (3, 11) and (9, 8)

4 (4, 0) and (12, 2)

5 (-3, 5) and (7, 1)

6 (2, -9) and (-4, 3)

7 (-6, -5) and (-2, 5)

8 (-4, 20) and (9, 3)

ISBN: 9780170354196

9 (-11, 0) and (2, -15)

10 (1, -7) and (-1, 10)

11 (1.75, 4.4) and (2.9, 7.8)

12 (-57, 91) and (18, -155)

13 Show that the following points are collinear: A (-5, 5), B (0, 3) and C (10, -1).

14 Show that the following points are collinear: A (-7, -11), B (123, 41) and C (188, 67).

ISBN: 9780170354196

Midpoints, distances and gradients

Calculate the midpoint, length and gradient for lines connecting these points.

1 (-7, -2) and (8, 4)

2 (-6, 3) and (2, -9)

3 (17, -1) and (-13, -6)

4 (-6, -11) and (2, 25)

ISBN: 9780170354196

5 (-10, -1) and (-2, -17)

6 (68, 45) and (-13, -20)

7 (-42, 91) and (112, -105)

8 (-221, 136) and (323, 68)

ISBN: 9780170354196

Parallel and perpendicular lines

Parallel lines have equal gradients. This means that $m_1 = m_2$

Parallel lines are like train tracks and will never cross one another.

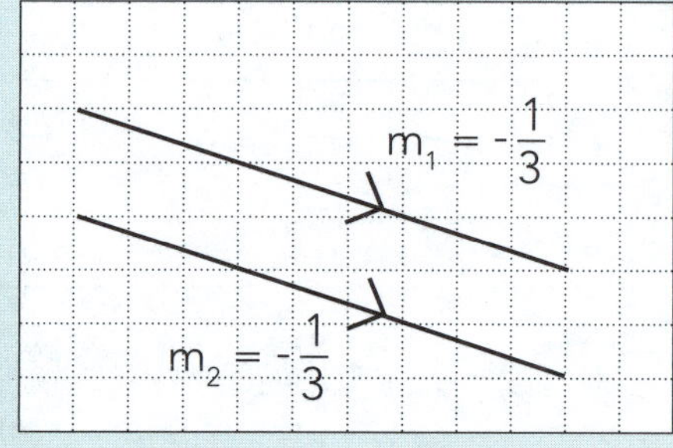

Perpendicular lines are at right angles to each other and they have gradients that are negative reciprocals of each other. This means that $m_1 \times m_2 = -1$

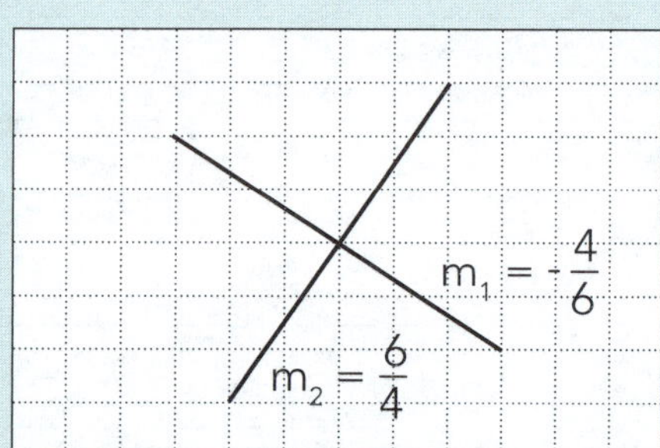

$$m_1 \times m_2 = -\frac{4}{6} \times \frac{6}{4}$$
$$= -1$$

1 Are the following lines parallel? Justify your answer with calculations.

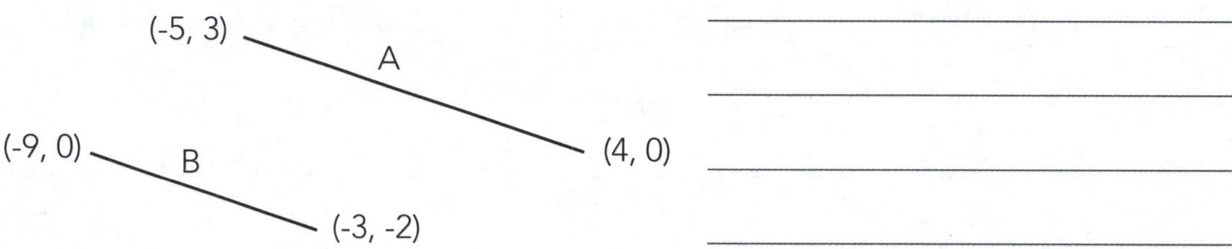

2 Are the following lines perpendicular? Justify your answer with calculations.

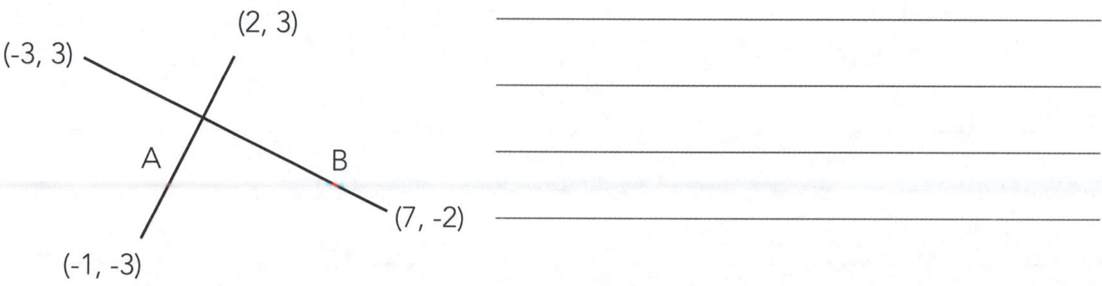

ISBN: 9780170354196

3 Calculate the gradients of these lines, then complete the table below.

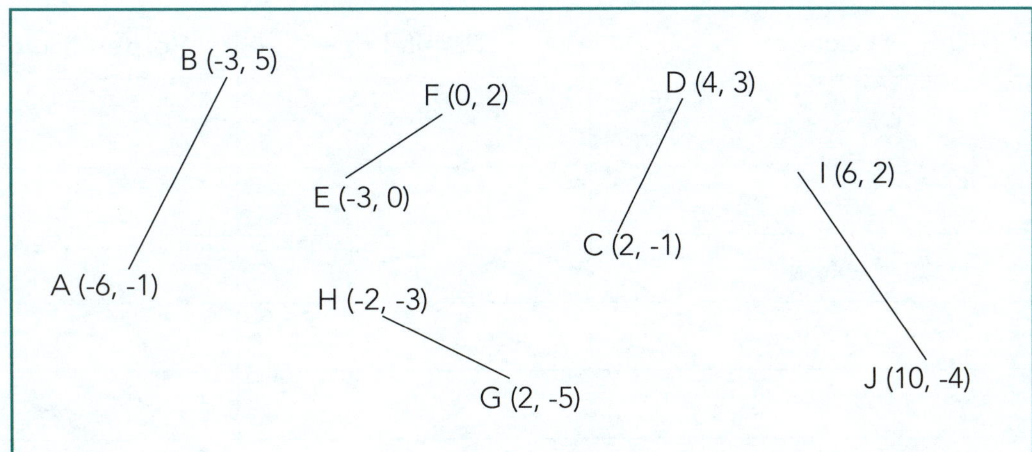

Line segment	Gradient	Parallel to ...	Perpendicular to ...
AB			
CD			
EF			
GH			
IJ			

4 Calculate the gradients of the following lines, and investigate whether they are parallel, perpendicular, or neither.

a Line A connects (-9, 3) and (11, -12)
Line B connects (11, -12) and (23, -2)

b Line C connects (-13, -2) and (5, 7)
Line D connects (-6, -12) and (12, -3)

ISBN: 9780170354196

5 Complete the table below.

	Equation	Parallel to	Perpendicular to
AB	$y = -\frac{5}{2}x - 5$		
CD	$2y = -5x + 4$		
EF	$y = 2.5x + 1$		
GH	$2x + 5y = -4$		
IJ	$10 + 2x = 5y$		

6 Is the triangle below right angled? Justify your answer using calculations.

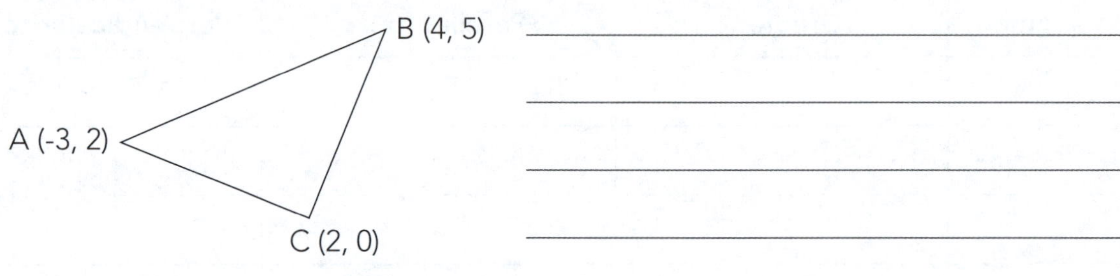

7 Calculate the value of p which would make these two lines parallel.
A: $-10y = 14x + 10$
B: $5y = px + 1$

8 Calculate the value of q which would make these two lines perpendicular.
A: $y = -1.4x - 1$
B: $7y = qx - 21$

ISBN: 9780170354196

9 The points A (-5, 2), B (14, 5) and C (9, -5) form the vertices of a triangle. Prove that this triangle is right angled:

a by calculating the lengths of the sides and using Pythagoras's theorem.

b by calculating the gradients of each side and showing that two sides are perpendicular.

10 The points A (-5, 10), B (7, 8) and C (-3, -2) form the vertices of a triangle.

a Calculate the length of each side and use these to show that this triangle is isosceles.

b Find the co-ordinates of two points that lie on the axis of symmetry for this triangle.

c Show that this axis of symmetry is perpendicular to one of the sides of the triangle.

ISBN: 9780170354196

Finding the equation of a straight line

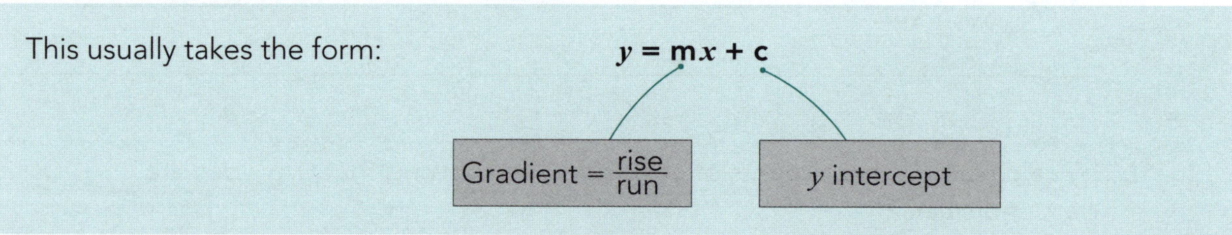

Using the gradient and the y intercept

Example:

1 From the graph,
$c = y$ intercept = -2

2 On the line, draw a right-angled triangle anywhere to find

$m = \text{gradient} = -\frac{6}{10} = -\frac{3}{5}$

3 Substitute these into $y = mx + c$ to get:

$y = -\frac{3}{5}x - 2$

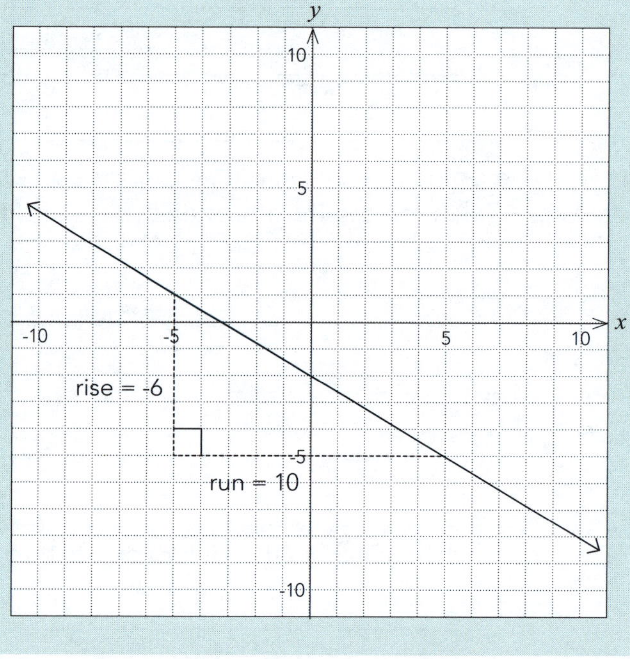

1 Complete the table.

Line	m	c	$y = mx + c$
———			
- - - - - -			
- - - - (teal)			
- — -			
——— (grey)			
——— (teal)			

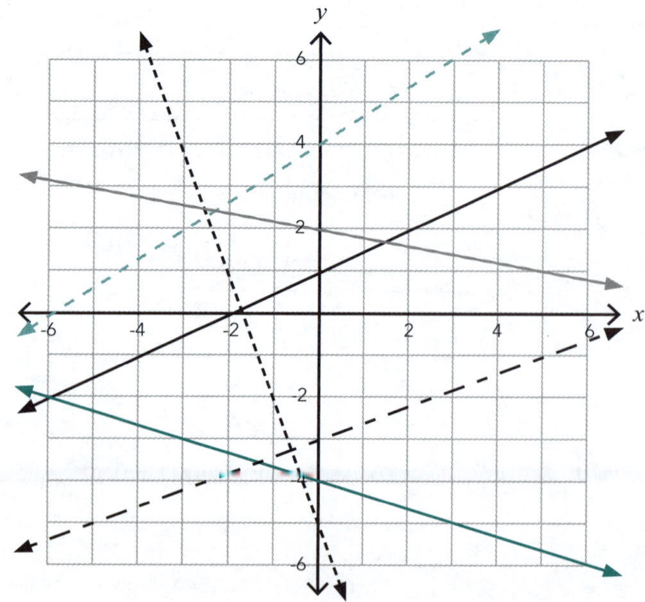

 ISBN: 9780170354196

2 Write down the equation of the line that passes through the point (0, 7) and which has a gradient of -3.

3 An equation with a gradient of 3.5 passes through the point (0, -2). Write down its equation.

4 A line passes through the origin and is parallel to the line $y = -5x + 17$. Write down its equation.

5 A line passes through the origin and is perpendicular to the line $y = 7x + 2$. Write down its equation.

6 Write down the equation of a line that passes through the point (0, -4) and is parallel to $y = \mathrm{p}x + 8$.

7 A line has a y intercept of 5 and is perpendicular to the line $3y = 2x - 9$. Write down its equation.

ISBN: 9780170354196

Using the gradient and one point

We use a different form of $y = \text{m}x + \text{c}$.
If the point is written (x_1, y_1), then $y - y_1 = \text{m}(x - x_1)$

Example: Find the equation of the line that passes through the point (4, -3) with the gradient $-\frac{1}{2}$.

$$(x_1, y_1) = (4, -3) \text{ so } x_1 = 4 \text{ and } y_1 = -3$$

$$y - (-3) = -\frac{1}{2}(x - 4)$$

$$y + 3 = -\frac{1}{2}x + 2$$

$$y = -\frac{1}{2}x - 1$$

Find equations for the following lines.

1 (2, 3) with a gradient of 3

2 (-4, 1) with a gradient of $-\frac{1}{2}$

3 (3, -5) with a gradient of 4

4 (1, 2) with a gradient of -3

5 (5, -2) with a gradient of -1

6 (-2, -3) with a gradient of $-\frac{1}{2}$

ISBN: 9780170354196

7 (8, -2) with a gradient of $\frac{3}{4}$

8 (-8, 2) with a gradient of $\frac{5}{8}$

9 (-1, -5) with a gradient of $\frac{5}{6}$

10 (-4, -3) with a gradient of $-\frac{2}{5}$

11 (2.5, -17.75) with a gradient of 0.1

12 (48, 60) with a gradient of 0.25

13 Find the equation of a line that is perpendicular to $5y = 4x + 3$ and which passes through the point (8, 13).

14 If a line with a gradient of m passes through the point (*a*, *b*), show that the y intercept (c) is $b - a\text{m}$.

ISBN: 9780170354196

Using two points

We use the same formula as above, but calculate the gradient first.
If the two points are (x_1, y_1) and (x_2, y_2), then:

$$m = \frac{y_2 - y_1}{x_2 - x_1} \quad \text{and} \quad y - y_1 = m(x - x_1)$$

Example: Find the equation of the line that passes through (4, -3) and (-6, 2).

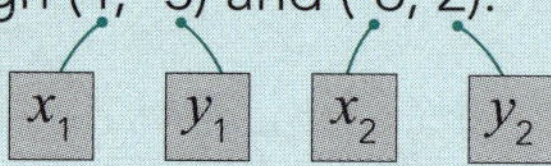

$$y - (-3) = \frac{2 - (-3)}{-6 - 4}(x - 4)$$

$$y + 3 = -\frac{5}{10}(x - 4)$$

$$y + 3 = -\frac{5}{10}x + 2$$

$$y = -\frac{1}{2}x - 1$$

Calculate the equations of the line that connects the following pairs of points.

1 (5, 8) and (7, 12)

2 (8, 2) and (2, 5)

3 (3, 11) and (9, 8)

4 (4, 0) and (12, 2)

 ISBN: 9780170354196

5 (-3, 5) and (6, 2)

6 (2, -9) and (-4, 3)

7 (-6, -5) and (-2, 5)

8 (-4, 20) and (1, 10)

9 (-8, -12) and (4, -21)

10 (1, -7) and (-1, 10)

11 (54, -78) and (-12, 32)

12 (0.5, -3.1) and (1.7, -5.5)

ISBN: 9780170354196

Putting it all together so far

1 Show that the points A (-2, 5), B (2, 3) and C (10, -1) lie on the same straight line and find the equation of the line.

2 Find the equation of a line that crosses the x-axis at 4 and the y-axis at -3.

3 A triangle has the vertices A (-3, 5), B (4, 2) and C (3, 7).

a Calculate the midpoint of side AC.

b Find the equation of the line that passes through this midpoint and point B.

4 Points A (-1, 2) and B (9, -2) form the diameter of a circle.

a Find the equation of the diameter.

ISBN: 9780170354196

b Calculate the co-ordinates of the centre of the circle.

c Calculate the length of the diameter.

5 The points A (-8, -5), B (-2, -9) and C (4, 0) form the vertices of a triangle.

a Find the gradient of each side, and use these to show that this is a right-angled triangle.

b Calculate the length of the hypotenuse.

6 Find the equations of the following three lines.

a Line A, which passes through (0, 91) with a gradient of $\frac{1}{3}$.

b Line B, which passes through the points (-117, -26) and (78, 65).

c Line C, which has a gradient of $\frac{1}{3}$ and passes through the point (-39, -78).

d Which of these lines are parallel? Justify your answer using the gradient of each.

7 a Find the equation of the line that passes through the points (-57, 152) and (114, -76).

b Show that the point (228, -228) lies on this line.

c Find the equation of the line that is perpendicular to your original line and which passes through the point (228, -228).

 ISBN: 9780170354196

Finding where two lines meet (their intersection)

This is found by solving the equations of the two lines simultaneously.
If these are given in $y = mx + c$ form, then make the two right-hand sides equal.

Example:
Find where the lines $y = 5x - 3$ and $y = -2x + 11$ meet.

$$\begin{aligned} \text{Since} \quad y &= y \\ \text{then} \quad 5x - 3 &= -2x + 11 \\ 7x &= 14 \\ x &= 2 \end{aligned}$$

Substitute for x into either equation:

$$\begin{aligned} y &= 5(2) - 3 \\ y &= 7 \end{aligned}$$

These two lines meet at (2, 7).

Find the co-ordinates of the points where the following lines meet.

1 $y = x + 2$ and $y = -2x + 8$

2 $y = x + 2$ and $y = -3x + 18$

3 $y = -x - 2$ and $y = -3x + 6$

4 $y = -2x + 7$ and $y = 3x + 2$

ISBN: 9780170354196

5 $y = \frac{1}{2}x + 4$ and $y = 3x - 1$

6 $y = -2x + 1$ and $y = \frac{3}{2}x - 6$

7 $y = -3x - 7$ and $y = 2$

8 $y = x - 7$ and $y = -\frac{2}{5}x$

9 $y = 0.75x - 4$ and $y = -2x + 7$

10 $y = \frac{5}{4}x - 7$ and $y = \frac{1}{2}x - 4$

11 $3y = -2x + 24$ and $3y - 5x = 3$

12 $5y - x = -40$ and $5y - 6x + 65 = 0$

ISBN: 9780170354196

Putting it together again

1 A triangle is formed by the lines:

A: $y = \frac{7}{4}x - 7\frac{1}{2}$

B: $y = -2x - 15$

and C: $y = \frac{1}{2}x + 5$

a By taking two equations at a time, find the co-ordinates of the corners of the triangle.

b Show that this triangle is right angled.

2 Show that the following points are collinear: A (-7, 10), B (9, 6) and C (17, 4).
Hint: Show that the gradients of each section are the same.

3 Find the equation of a line that passes through the point (6, 1) and is parallel to the line that passes through the points A (0, -5) and B (10, -3).

4 Calculate the gradient and the y intercept of the line $3x - 5y + 13 = 0$.

ISBN: 9780170354196

5 The points A (1, 11), B (-5, 3) and C (3, -3) form the vertices of a triangle.

a Calculate the length of each side in order to show that the triangle is isosceles.

b Find the gradients of each side in order to show that the triangle is right angled.

c Calculate the midpoints of lines AB and BC.

d Use these, along with the gradients you found in **b**, to find the equations of the perpendicular bisectors of AB and BC.

e Show that these perpendicular bisectors meet at the midpoint of the line AC.

6 AB is a line segment that has A (-5, 9) and a midpoint (5, 5).
Calculate the co-ordinates of B.

ISBN: 9780170354196

7 A triangle has vertices A (-3, 7), B (-1, 1) and C (11, 5).

a Show that this triangle is scalene.

b Show that it is a right-angled triangle.

8 The vertices of a triangle are A (-3, 6), B (-5, -11) and C (7, -7).

a Calculate the length of BC.

b Find the midpoint of BC.

c Find the equation of the line that passes through A and bisects the line BC.

9 A triangle is formed by the following lines:

A $7y = -11x - 7$

B $y = \frac{3}{7}x - 1$

C $7y = -4x - 56$

Calculate the co-ordinates of the vertices of the triangle.

ISBN: 9780170354196

Properties of quadrilaterals

Make your own summary of the properties of quadrilaterals:

Name	Diagram	Angles?	Side lengths?	Sides parallel?	Diagonals?
Square				Two pairs, opposite each other.	
Rhombus			Four equal.		Not equal, perpendicular, both bisect each other.
Rectangle		Four right angles.			Equal, not perpendicular, both bisect each other.
Parallelogram			Opposite sides equal, adjacent sides not.	Two pairs, opposite each other.	
Kite			Two pairs of equal sides, adjacent to each other.		Not equal, perpendicular, one pair bisected by the other.
Trapezium			None		
Isosceles trapezium		Two adjacent pairs, equal angles, no right angles.			Equal, not perpendicular, do not bisect each other.

ISBN: 9780170354196

Quadrilateral practice

1 ABCD is a parallelogram with its vertices labelled clockwise, and in alphabetical order. They are A (3, -9), B (-3, -3), C (9, -1) and D (x, y).

a Sketch these points.

b Calculate the gradients of AB and BC.

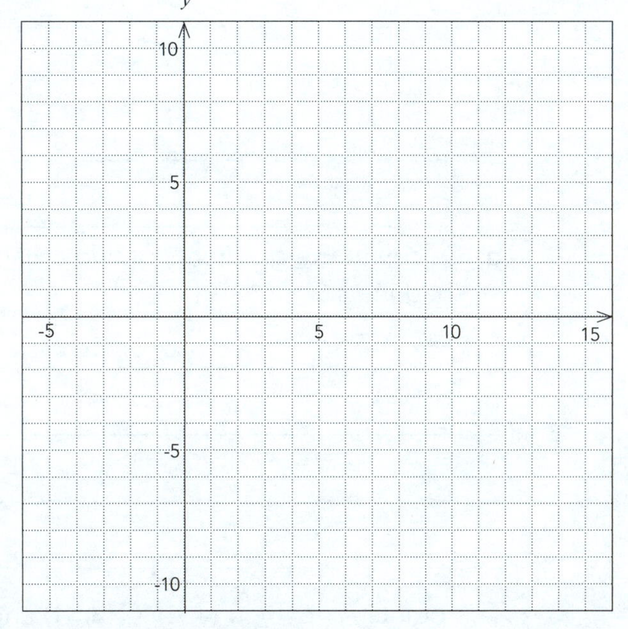

c Use these to help you find the equations of sides AD and CD.

d Use these equations to calculate the co-ordinates of D.

e Calculate the lengths of the diagonals, AC and BD.

f Calculate the gradients of the diagonals, and use these to show that AC and BD are not perpendicular.

ISBN: 9780170354196

2 The points A (-3, 5), B (7, 7), C (5, -3) and D (-5, -5) form the vertices of a quadrilateral.

a By calculating the length of each side, show that this must be either a rhombus or a square.

b Calculate the gradients of two adjacent sides, and use these to determine which shape it is.

3 The points A (-6, 8), B (4, 4), C (2, -1) and D (-8, 3) form the vertices of a quadrilateral.

a Calculate the length of each side.

b Calculate the lengths of the diagonals.

c Calculate the gradients of the diagonals.

d What type of quadrilateral is this? Use your answers from the previous questions to justify this.

ISBN: 9780170354196

4 Points A (-26, 117), B (39, 156), C (78, 91) and D (-13, -52) form the corners of a quadrilateral.

a Calculate the length of each side.

b Calculate the lengths of the diagonals.

c Show that the diagonals intersect at right angles.

d Calculate the co-ordinates of the point (X) where the diagonals meet.

e Show that point X bisects the line AC.

f What sort of quadrilateral do these points form? Use any of your answers above to prove this.

ISBN: 9780170354196

Centres of triangles

1 **Median**: Joins the centre of a side to the opposite vertex.

Centroid: The point at which medians meet.

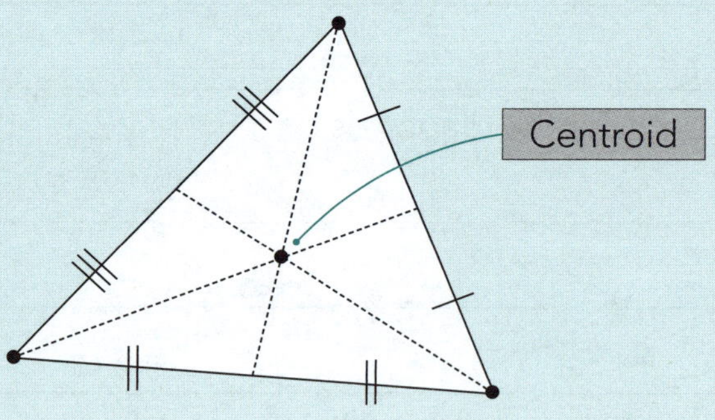

2 **Mediator**: The perpendicular bisector of a side.

Circumcentre: The point at which the mediators meet. A circle can be drawn from this which passes through all three vertices of the triangle.

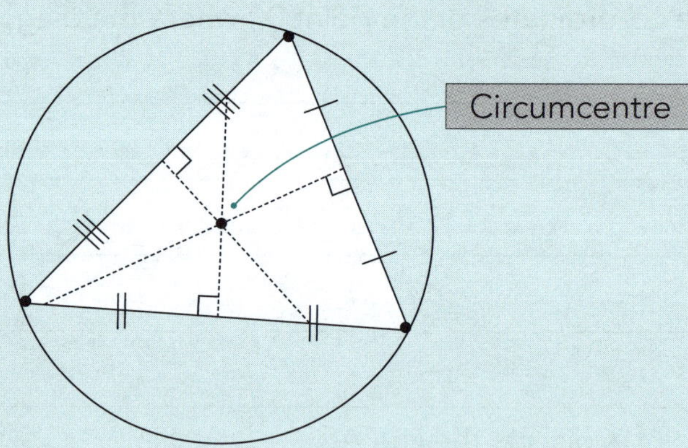

3 **Altitude**: Line that is perpendicular to a side and which passes through the opposite vertex.

Orthocentre: The point where the altitudes meet.

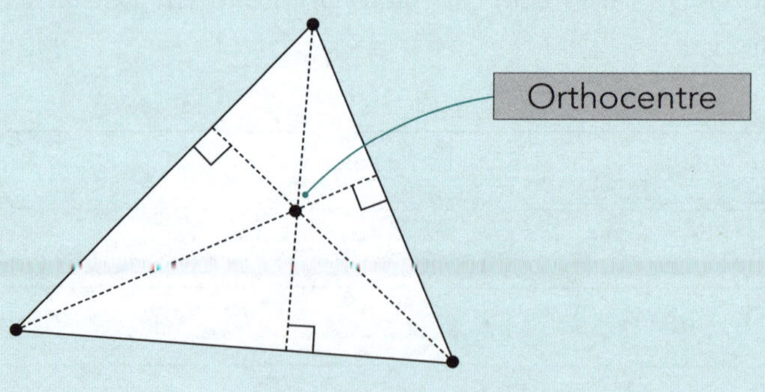

ISBN: 9780170354196

Triangle practice

1 The vertices of a triangle are A (-5, -1), B (1, 5) and C (7, -1).

a Calculate the midpoints of each side.

b Calculate the equations of the medians of the triangle (these connect each midpoint with the opposite vertex).

c Solve two of these equations simultaneously in order to find the co-ordinates of the centroid (where the medians meet).

2 The vertices of a triangle are A (-1, -3), B (1, 3) and C (5, -3).

a Calculate the gradient of each side.

b Calculate the midpoint of each side.

ISBN: 9780170354196

c Use the midpoints and the gradients to help you to calculate the equations of the mediators of sides AB and BC.

d By solving two of these equations simultaneously, calculate the co-ordinates of the circumcentre of this triangle.

3 The vertices of a triangle are the same as in question **2**: A (-1, -3), B (1, 3) and C (5, -3).

a Using the gradient of AB along with the co-ordinates of point C, calculate the equation of the altitude from AB to point C.

b Using the gradient of BC along with the co-ordinates of point A, calculate the equation of the altitude from BC to point A.

c Solve these equations simultaneously in order to calculate the co-ordinates of the orthocentre of this triangle.

ISBN: 9780170354196

Practice tasks

Practice task one

Calculate the gradients and the lengths of the lines connecting these points, and use these to prove that this is a right-angled isosceles triangle.

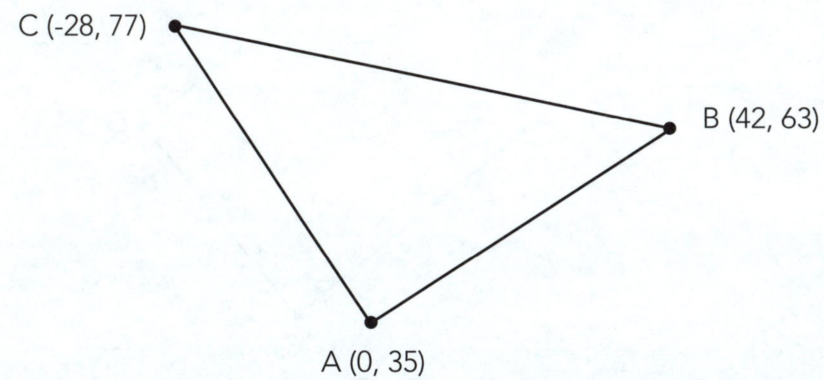

ISBN: 9780170354196

Practice task two

Calculate the midpoints, gradients and the lengths of the two diagonals, and use these to prove that this figure is a rectangle.

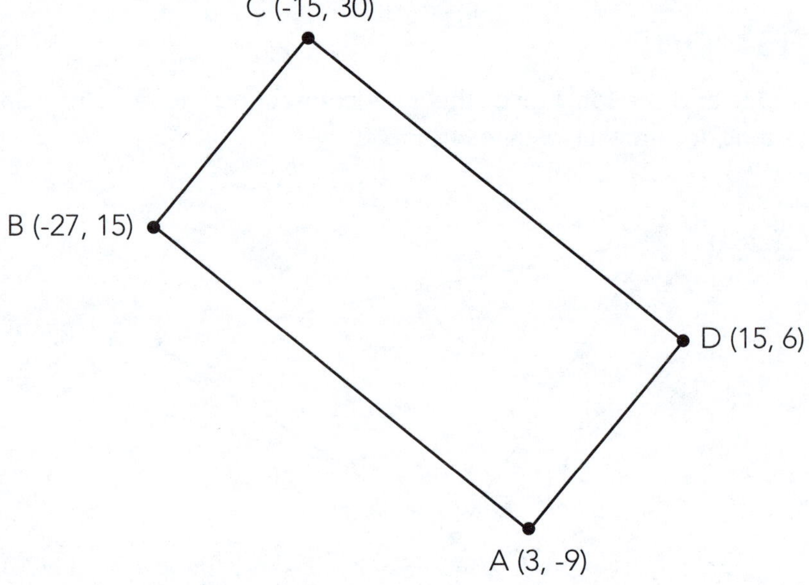

 ISBN: 9780170354196

Practice task three

Calculate the gradients and the lengths of the lines connecting these points, and use these to find out what type of triangle this is (equilateral, isosceles or scalene) and whether it is right angled.

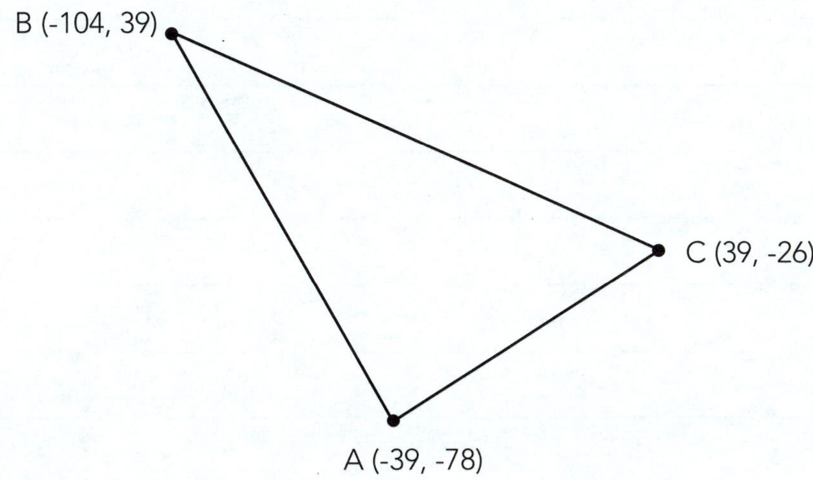

ISBN: 9780170354196

Practice task four

The vertices of a quadrilateral are A (-102, 68), B (51, 102), C (170, 0) and D (17, -34).

Calculate the lengths and gradients of its sides and diagonals. Use these to prove what type of quadrilateral it is.

ISBN: 9780170354196

Practice task five

Prove that the four points A (15, 0), B (30, -15), C (-15, -10) and D (-30, 5) are the vertices of a parallelogram. Find the equations of the diagonals, and use these to calculate the co-ordinates of the point where these meet.

ISBN: 9780170354196

Practice task six

The vertices of a triangle are A (-26, -52), B (-52, 78) and C (78, 52).

Calculate the midpoints of the sides of this triangle, and use these to find the equations of the mediators. Calculate the co-ordinates of the point where the mediators meet (the circumcentre).

ISBN: 9780170354196

Practice task seven

The vertices of a triangle are A (42, -7), B (14, 21) and C (42, 35).

Calculate the midpoints and gradients of the sides of this triangle, and use these to find the equations of the medians. Calculate the co-ordinates of the point where the medians meet (the centroid).

ISBN: 9780170354196

Practice task eight

Calculate gradients and lengths in order to prove that A (10, -4), B (-6, 8) and C (6, 24) are three vertices of a square. Calculate the co-ordinates of the fourth vertex.

 ISBN: 9780170354196

Answers

All non-integral intermediate answers are rounded to 4 sf.
All non-integral final answers are rounded to 3 sf.
Professional judgement should apply.

Co-ordinates revision (pp. 7–8)

A (4, 3)
B (3, 0)
C (1, 9)
D (8, -2)
E (-6, 3)
F (0, 0)
G (-3, -2)
H (10, 8)
I (-9, 0)
J (-10, 5)
K (5, -6)
L (-8, -9)
M (0, -8)
N (9, -7)
O (-4, 7)
P (-9, -4)

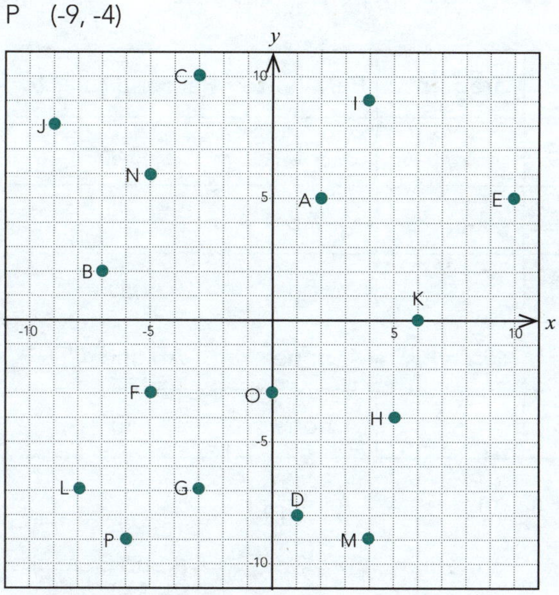

Midpoints (pp. 9–11)

1 (6, 10)
2 (5, 4)
3 (6, 9.5)
4 (8, 1)
5 (2, 3)
6 (-1, -3)
7 (-4, 0)
8 (2.5, 11.5)
9 (-4.5, -7.5)
10 (0, 1.5)
11 (3.75, 1.75)
12 (-6.8, -1.7)
13 (1, -2)
14 PQ: (-2, 4)
QR: (4, 2)
PR: (0, -1)
15 (1, -0.5)
16 (11, 11)
17 $p = -76$
$q = -133$
18 $e = -117$
$g = 28$
$h = 39$

The distance between two points (pp. 12–14)

1 4.47
2 8.94
3 6.71
4 8.25
5 10.8
6 13.4
7 10.8
8 21.4
9 19.8
10 17.1
11 3.59
12 257
13 AB = BC = 11.4
AC = 16.1
∴ isosceles
14 7.62
15 **a** OK = OM = ON = 5
OL = 5.66
∴ L not on circle
b d = 10 units
16 AB = 175
BC = 293
AC = 228
∴ scalene
17 $y = 0$ or -6
18 65

ISBN: 9780170354196

The gradient of a line (pp. 15–19)

A $\frac{3}{2}$ B 2

C $\frac{1}{5}$ D 0

E $-\frac{3}{4}$ F $-\frac{5}{2}$

G 1 H Undefined

I $\frac{2}{3}$ J $-\frac{1}{7}$

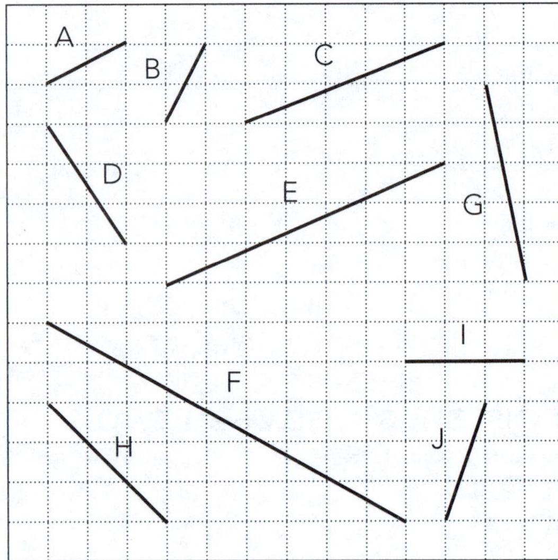

Calculating the gradient (pp. 18–19)

1 2

2 $\frac{1}{2}$

3 $-\frac{1}{2}$

4 $\frac{1}{4}$

5 $-\frac{2}{5}$

6 -2

7 $\frac{5}{2}$

8 $-\frac{17}{13}$

9 $-\frac{15}{13}$

10 $-\frac{17}{2}$

11 2.96

12 -3.28

13 AB = $-\frac{2}{5}$, BC = $-\frac{4}{10} = -\frac{2}{5}$ ∴ collinear

14 AB = $\frac{2}{5}$, BC = $\frac{2}{5}$ ∴ collinear

Midpoints, distances and gradients (pp. 20–21)

1 Mid: $(\frac{1}{2}, 1)$ l = 16.2 m = $\frac{2}{5}$

2 Mid: (-2, -3) l = 14.4 m = $-\frac{3}{2}$

3 Mid: $(2, \frac{-7}{2})$ l = 30.4 m = $\frac{1}{6}$

4 Mid: (-2, 7) l = 36.9 m = $\frac{9}{2}$

5 Mid: (-6, -9) l = 17.9 m = -2

6 Mid: (27.5, 12.5) l = 104 m = 0.8025

7 Mid: (35, -7) l = 249 m = $-\frac{14}{11}$

8 Mid: (51, 102) l = 548 m = $-\frac{1}{8}$

Parallel and perpendicular lines (pp. 22–25)

1 A: $\frac{3}{-9} = -\frac{1}{3}$ B: $\frac{3}{-9} = -\frac{1}{3}$

Gradients are both $-\frac{1}{3}$ so they are parallel.

2 A: $\frac{6}{3} = 2$ B: $-\frac{5}{10} = -\frac{1}{2}$

$m_A \times m_B = 2 \times -\frac{1}{2} = -1$

so A and B are perpendicular.

3

	Gradient	Parallel to	Perpendicular to
AB	$\frac{6}{3} = 2$	CD	GH
CD	$\frac{4}{2} = 2$	AB	GH
EF	$\frac{2}{3}$	none	IJ
GH	$\frac{2}{-4} = -\frac{1}{2}$	none	AB and CD
IJ	$-\frac{3}{2}$	none	EF

4 a $m_A = -\frac{3}{4}$ $m_B = \frac{10}{12}$

$m_A \times m_B = -\frac{3}{4} \times \frac{10}{12} \neq -1 \Rightarrow$ A and B are not perpendicular

$m_A \neq m_B \Rightarrow$ A and B are not parallel

∴ neither

b $m_C = \frac{1}{2}$ $m_D = \frac{1}{2}$

$m_C \times m_D = \frac{1}{2} \times \frac{1}{2} \neq -1 \Rightarrow$ C and D are not perpendicular

∴ $m_C = m_D \Rightarrow$ A and B are parallel

ISBN: 9780170354196

5

	Gradient	Parallel to	Perpendicular to
AB	$-\frac{5}{2}$	CD	IJ
CD	$-\frac{5}{2}$	AB	IJ
EF	$\frac{5}{2}$	none	GH
GH	$-\frac{2}{5}$	none	EF
IJ	$\frac{2}{5}$	none	AB and CD

6 A: $\frac{6}{3} = 2$ B: $-\frac{4}{10} = -\frac{1}{2}$

$m_{BC} \times m_{AC} = \frac{5}{2} \times -\frac{2}{5} = -1$ so BC and AC are perpendicular

∴ right-angled Δ

7 $m_A = -\frac{7}{5}$ ∴ $m_B = -\frac{7}{5}$

So p = -7

8 $m_A = -1.4 = -\frac{7}{5}$ ∴ $m_B = \frac{5}{7}$

So q = 5

9 a AB = 19.24

BC = 11.18

CA = 15.65

$11.18^2 + 15.65^2 = 370$

$19.24^2 = 370$

∴ $BC^2 + CA^2 = AB^2$ so Δ must be right angled.

b $m_{AB} = \frac{3}{19}$, $m_{BC} = \frac{10}{5} = 2$, $m_{AC} = -\frac{7}{14} = -\frac{1}{2}$

∴ $m_{BC} \times m_{AC} = 2 \times -\frac{1}{2} = -1$

∴ BC and AC are perpendicular so Δ must be right angled.

10 a AB = 12.2

BC = 14.1

CA = 12.2

∴ Δ must be isosceles.

b Midpoint BC = (2, 3)

∴ axis of symmetry passes through (-5, 10) and (2, 3)

c $m_{axis} = -\frac{7}{7} = -1$

$m_{CB} = \frac{10}{10} = 1$

∴ $m_{axis} \times m_{CB} = -1$ so axis and CB are perpendicular.

Finding the equation of a straight line (pp. 26–31)

Using the gradient and the *y* intercept (pp. 26–27)

1

Line	m	c	$y = mx + c$
——	$\frac{1}{2}$	+1	$y = \frac{1}{2}x + 1$
------	-3	-5	$y = -3x - 5$
- - - -	$\frac{2}{3}$	+4	$y = \frac{2}{3}x + 4$
- — -	$\frac{2}{5}$	-3	$y = \frac{2}{5}x - 3$
——	$-\frac{1}{5}$	+2	$y = -\frac{1}{5}x + 2$
——	$-\frac{1}{3}$	-4	$y = -\frac{1}{3}x - 4$

2 $y = -3x + 7$

3 $y = \frac{7}{2}x - 2$

4 $y = -5x$

5 $y = -\frac{1}{7}x$

6 $y = px - 4$

7 $y = -\frac{3}{2}x + 5$

Using the gradient and one point (pp. 28–29)

1 $y = 3x - 3$

2 $y = \frac{1}{2}x - 1$

3 $y = 4x - 17$

4 $y = -3x + 5$

5 $y = -x + 3$

6 $y = -\frac{1}{2}x - 4$

7 $y = \frac{3}{4}x - 8$

8 $y = \frac{5}{8}x + 7$

9 $y = \frac{5}{6}x - \frac{25}{6}$

10 $y = -\frac{2}{5}x - \frac{23}{5}$

11 $y = 0.1x - 18$

12 $y = 0.25x + 48$

13 $y = -\frac{5}{4}x + 23$

14 $y - b = m(x - a) \Rightarrow y = mx - am + b \Rightarrow$ $c = b - am$

ISBN: 9780170354196

Using two points (pp. 30–31)

1 $y = 2x - 2$

2 $y = -\frac{1}{2}x + 6$

3 $y = -\frac{1}{2}x + 12\frac{1}{2}$

4 $y = \frac{1}{4}x - 1$

5 $y = -\frac{1}{3}x + 4$

6 $y = -2x - 5$

7 $y = 2.5x + 10$

8 $y = -2x + 12$

9 $y = -\frac{3}{4}x - 18$

10 $y = -\frac{17}{2}x + 1\frac{1}{2}$

11 $y = -\frac{5}{3}x + 12$

12 $y = -2x - 2.1$

Putting it all together so far (pp. 32–34)

1 $m_{AB} = -\frac{1}{2}$ $m_{BC} = -\frac{1}{2}$

∴ A, B and C are on the same line.

Equation: $y = -\frac{1}{2}x + 4$

2 $m = \frac{3}{4}$

Equation: $y = \frac{3}{4}x - 3$

3 **a** (0, 6)
b $y = -x + 6$

4 **a** $y = -\frac{2}{5}x + \frac{8}{5}$
b (4, 0)
c 10.8

5 **a** AB: $-\frac{2}{3}$ BC: $\frac{3}{2}$ AC: $\frac{5}{12}$

$m_{AB} \times m_{BC} = -\frac{2}{3} \times \frac{3}{2} = -1$

so BC and AC are perpendicular

∴ right-angled Δ

b 13

6 **a** $y = \frac{1}{3}x + 91$
b $y = \frac{7}{15}x + 28.6$
c $y = \frac{1}{3}x - 65$
d A and C are parallel because both their gradients are $\frac{1}{3}$

7 **a** $y = -\frac{4}{3}x + 76$
b $-\frac{4}{3} \times 228 + 76 = -228$

∴ The point lies on the line

c $y = \frac{3}{4}x - 399$

Finding where two lines meet (their intersection) (pp. 35–36)

1 (2, 4)
2 (4, 6)
3 (4, -6)
4 (1, 5)
5 (2, 5)
6 (2, -3)
7 (-3, 2)
8 (5, -2)
9 (4, -1)
10 (4, -2)
11 (3, 6)
12 (5, -7)

Putting it together again (pp. 37–39)

1 **a** (-2, -11), (-8, 1), (10, 10)
b $m_B \times m_C = -2 \times \frac{1}{2} = -1$

so BC and AC are perpendicular
∴ right-angled Δ

2 $m_{AB} = -\frac{1}{4}$ $m_{BC} = -\frac{1}{4}$ $m_{AC} = -\frac{1}{4}$

∴ A, B and C are collinear

3 $y = \frac{1}{5}x - \frac{1}{5}$

4 $m = \frac{3}{5}$ $c = \frac{13}{5}$

5 **a** $l_{AB} = 10$
$l_{CB} = 10$
$l_{AC} = 14.14$

so Δ is isosceles

b $m_{AB} \times m_{BC} = \frac{4}{3} \times -\frac{3}{4} = -1$

so AB and BC are perpendicular
∴ right-angled Δ

c $\text{Midpoint}_{AB} = (-2, 7)$
$\text{Midpoint}_{BC} = (-1, 0)$

d $\text{Perpendicular bisector}_{AB}$ is $y = -\frac{3}{4}x + \frac{11}{2}$

$\text{Perpendicular bisector}_{BC}$ is $y = \frac{4}{3}x + \frac{4}{3}$

e AB: midpoint = (2, 4)

$-\frac{3}{4}x + \frac{11}{2} = \frac{4}{3}x + \frac{4}{3} \Rightarrow x = 2$ and $y = 4$

6 (15, 1)

 ISBN: 9780170354196

7 a $l_{AB} = 6.32$ $l_{CB} = 12.7$ $l_{AC} = 14.1$

∴ all lengths are different so Δ is scalene

b Either by Pythagoras:

$6.32^2 + 12.65^2 = 199.96 = 14.14^2$

Or $m_{AB} \times m_{BC} = -3 \times \frac{1}{3} = -1$

so AB and BC are perpendicular

∴ right-angled Δ

8 a $l_{BC} = 12.65$

b $\text{midpoint}_{BC} = (1, -9)$

c $y = -\frac{15}{4}x - \frac{21}{4}$

9 (0, -1), (-7, -4), (7, -12)

Properties of quadrilaterals (pp. 40–43)

Quadrilateral practice (pp. 41–43)

1 b $m_{AB} = -1$ $m_{BC} = \frac{1}{6}$

c AD: $y = \frac{1}{6}x - 9.5$

CD: $y = -x + 8$

d (15, -7)

e $l_{AC} = 10$ $l_{BD} = 18.44$

f $m_{AC} = \frac{4}{3}$ $m_{BD} = -\frac{2}{9}$

∴ $m_{AC} \times m_{BD} = \frac{4}{3} \times -\frac{2}{9} \neq -1 \Rightarrow$ AC and BD are not perpendicular

2 a $l_{AB} = l_{BC} = l_{CD} = l_{AC} = 10.20$

b $m_{AB} = \frac{1}{5}$ $m_{BC} = 5$

∴ $m_{AB} \times m_{BC} = \frac{1}{5} \times 5 \neq -1 \Rightarrow$ AB and BC are not perpendicular

∴ This figure is a rhombus

3 a $l_{AB} = l_{DC} = 10.8$

$l_{BC} = l_{AD} = 5.39$

b $l_{AC} = l_{BD} = 12.0$

c $m_{AC} = -\frac{9}{8}$ $m_{BD} = \frac{1}{12}$

d Opposite sides are equal to each other, but adjacent sides are different, so figure must be a rectangle or parallelogram. Diagonals are equal, so is a rectangle.

4 a $l_{AB} = l_{BC} = 75.8$

$l_{CD} = l_{AD} = 170$

b $l_{AC} = 107$ $l_{BD} = 214$

c $m_{AC} \times m_{BD} = -\frac{1}{4} \times 4 = -1$

so AC and BD are perpendicular

d Equation AC: $y = -\frac{1}{4}x + 111$

Equation BD: $y = 4x$

Solving these simultaneously, they meet at (26, 104)

e Midpoint of AC is

$\left(\frac{-23 + 78}{2}, \frac{117 + 91}{2}\right) = (26, 104)$

or $l_{AX} = l_{XC} = 53.6$

f $l_{AB} = l_{BC}$ and $l_{CD} = l_{AD}$ so there are two pairs of adjacent equal sides.

Diagonals AC and BD are perpendicular.

Therefore the figure is a kite.

Centres of triangles (pp. 44–46)

Triangle practice (pp. 45–46)

1 a AB: (-2, 2)

BC: (4, 2)

AC: (1, -1)

b Med AB passes through (-2, 2) and (7, -1):

$y = -\frac{1}{3}x + \frac{4}{3}$

Med BC passes through (4, 2) and (-5, -1):

$y = \frac{1}{3}x + \frac{2}{3}$

Med AB passes through (1, -1) and (1, 5):

$x = 1$

c Centroid: (1, 1)

2 a $m_{AB} = 3$ $m_{BC} = -\frac{3}{2}$ $m_{AC} = 0$

b $\text{Midpoint}_{AB} = (0, 0)$

$\text{Midpoint}_{BC} = (3, 0)$

$\text{Midpoint}_{AC} = (2, -3)$

c Mediator_{AB}: $y = -\frac{1}{3}x$

Mediator_{BC}: $y = \frac{2}{3}x - 2$

d Circumcentre: $(2, -\frac{2}{3})$

3 a $m_{AB} = 3 \Rightarrow$ gradient of altitude $= -\frac{1}{3}$

Equation: $y = -\frac{1}{3}x - \frac{4}{3}$

b $m_{BC} = -\frac{3}{2} \Rightarrow$ gradient of altitude $= \frac{2}{3}$

Equation: $y = \frac{2}{3}x + \frac{7}{3}$

c Orthocentre: $(1, -\frac{5}{3})$

Practice tasks (pp. 47–54)

Practice task one (p. 47)

$m_{AB} = \frac{2}{3}$ $m_{BC} = -\frac{1}{5}$ $m_{AC} = -\frac{3}{2}$

$l_{AB} = 50.48$ $l_{BC} = 71.39$ $l_{AC} = 50.48$

$l_{AB} = l_{AC} \neq l_{BC} \Rightarrow$ triangle is isosceles

Either by Pythagoras:

$50.48^2 + 50.48^2 = 5096.53 = 71.39^2$

or $m_{AB} \times m_{AC} = \frac{2}{3} \times -\frac{3}{2} = -1$

so AB and AC are perpendicular ∴ right-angled Δ

ISBN: 9780170354196

Practice task two (p. 48)

$mid_{AC} = (-6, 10.5)$
$mid_{BD} = (-6, 10.5)$
$m_{AC} = -\frac{13}{6}$
$m_{BD} = -\frac{3}{14}$
$l_{AC} = 43.0$
$l_{BD} = 43.0$
The diagonals are equal and they bisect each other, but not at right angles ∴ the figure is a rectangle.

Practice task three (p. 49)

$m_{AB} = -\frac{117}{65}$ $m_{BC} = -\frac{65}{143}$ $m_{AC} = \frac{52}{78}$
$l_{AB} = 134$ $l_{CB} = 157$ $l_{AC} = 93.7$
$m_{AB} \times m_{AC} = -\frac{117}{65} \times \frac{52}{78} = 1.2 \neq -1$
so AB and AC are not perpendicular ∴ not a right-angled Δ. The lengths of all the sides are different so this is a scalene triangle.

Practice task four (p. 50)

$l_{AB} = l_{BC} = l_{CD} = l_{AC} = 157$
$l_{AC} = 280$
$l_{BD} = 140$
$m_{AC} \times m_{BD} = -\frac{1}{4} \times 4 = -1$ so AC and BD are perpendicular.
Equal sides along with unequal but perpendicular diagonals mean that this figure is a rhombus.

Practice task five (p. 51)

$l_{AB} = 21.2$ $m_{AB} = -1$
$l_{BC} = 45.3$ $m_{BC} = -\frac{1}{9}$
$l_{CD} = 21.2$ $m_{CD} = -1$
$l_{AD} = 45.3$ $m_{AD} = -\frac{1}{9}$
Opposite sides are equal ($l_{AB} = l_{CD} = 21.2$ and $l_{BC} = l_{AD} = 45.3$) and parallel ($m_{AB} = m_{CD} = -1$ and $m_{BC} = m_{AD} = -\frac{1}{9}$), but not perpendicular ($\frac{1}{9} \times -1 \neq -1$).
∴ A, B, C and D are the vertices of a parallelogram
$m_{AC} = \frac{1}{3} \Rightarrow$ Equation: $y = \frac{1}{3}x - 5$
$m_{BD} = -\frac{1}{3} \Rightarrow$ Equation: $y = -\frac{1}{3}x - 5$
∴ both have the same y intercept, so they meet at (0, -5)

Practice task six (p. 52)

$m_{AB} = -5$ $mid_{AB} = (-39, 13)$
$m_{BC} = -\frac{1}{5}$ $mid_{BC} = (13, 65)$
$m_{CA} = 1$ $mid_{CA} = (26, 0)$
Equations of mediators:
AB: $m = \frac{1}{5} \Rightarrow y = \frac{1}{5}x + 20.8$
BC: $m = 5 \Rightarrow y = 5x$
AC: $m = -1 \Rightarrow y = -x + 26$
Solve any two of these simultaneously
⇒ circumcentre is (4.33, 21.67)

Practice task seven (p. 53)

$mid_{AB} = (28, 7)$
$mid_{BC} = (28, 28)$
$mid_{AC} = (42, 14)$

$med_{AB\to C}$: Passes through (28, 7), (42, 35)
$m = 2 \Rightarrow y = 2x - 49$
$med_{BC\to A}$: Passes through (28, 28), (42, -7)
$m = -\frac{5}{2} \Rightarrow y = -\frac{5}{2}x + 98$
$med_{AC\to B}$: Passes through (42, 14), (14, 21)
$m = -\frac{1}{4} \Rightarrow y = -\frac{1}{4}x + 24.5$

Solve any two of these ⇒ centroid (32.7, 16.3)

Practice task eight (p. 54)

$l_{AB} = l_{BC} = 20$
$m_{AB} \times m_{BC} = -\frac{3}{4} \times \frac{4}{3} = -1$ so AB and BC are perpendicular.

Since AB and BC are equal and perpendicular, they can form three of the corners of a square.
Equation of AD:
$m_{AD} = \frac{4}{3}$ (parallel to BC) and passes through (10, -4)
$\Rightarrow y = \frac{4}{3}x - \frac{52}{3}$
Equation of DC:
$m_{DC} = -\frac{3}{4}$ (parallel to BC) and passes through (6, 24)
$\Rightarrow y = -\frac{3}{4}x + \frac{57}{2}$
Solving these simultaneously, D is (22, 12).

ISBN: 9780170354196